Help! My Debt is Making Me Miserable

Tips to help you Confront Your Finances, Reduce Your Expenses and Increase Your Income

Richard G Lowe, Jr

Help! My Debt is Making Me Miserable

Tips to help you Confront Your Finances, Reduce Your Expenses and Increase Your Income

Personal Finance Series #1

Published by The Writing King
www.thewritingking.com

Help! My Debt is Making Me Miserable

Copyright © 2016 by Richard G Lowe, Jr.

Cover Artist: theamateurzone

ASIN: B01M1AKGPM
ISBN: 978-1-943517-65-7 (Hardcover)
ISBN: 978-1-943517-64-0 (Paperback)
ISBN: 978-1-943517-63-3 (eBook)

Table of Contents

Table of Contents

Introduction

I am not a lawyer, a credit counselor, or an accountant. Depending on your situation, you should seek the help of qualified professionals as needed before taking any of the steps that I've outlined or discussed in this book.

It seems these days that everyone gets themselves in debt in one way or another. In modern times it's difficult not to accumulate some debt, if only for the purchase of a house or car.

In actuality, there is nothing wrong with carrying a bit of debt through your life. Few have the luxury of being able to afford to purchase a house with cash, or to buy a car out right without using credit. In fact, most people can't buy furniture or a refrigerator or other large purchases without using some kind of credit.

Not buying anything on credit actually, puts you at a disadvantage, and makes it difficult to get credit if you need it. It's hard to prove that you are credit worthy if you don't have any credit record at all.

That's why it is a good idea to purchase a car, some furniture, or a home on credit. This establishes you, assuming you keep up the payments, as someone who can be trusted with credit. If you pay regularly without being late, you'll build a record as a person who can be trusted. This can take several years, but it's worth the effort.

Introduction

Even carrying a credit card or two, and using them now and again, is not a problem as long as you keep it under control. It's wise to keep a general credit card, gas card, and perhaps a store credit card with you.

The best practice is to be able to pay off the entire balance of all your credit cards each month. Most people can't or don't do that, of course, but you should be able to pay them off within a reasonable amount of time, say within six months or a year.

Credit becomes a problem if you have difficulty making the payments each month. There are also other measures that are used to determine when it becomes an issue, various ratios of debt to how much you make in a year.

You know you are beginning to have a problem with your debt if any of the following are true.

 If your credit cards are maxed out, meaning they are at or even over the credit limit.

 If your credit cards have high interest rates, generally anything double-digit.

 If you are denied credit because you have too much credit.

 If you are unable to make payments because you don't have enough income.

 If you're using one credit card to pay another.

 If you have a lot of credit but don't have any savings.

If you're only making the minimum payments on your cards each month.

If you are late in paying your bills, credit cards, mortgage, rent, utilities and anything else.

If you're bouncing checks or overdrawing your checking account.

If you're having to choose between paying rent, utilities, groceries, bills, car payments and the mortgage each month.

If you're receiving harassing phone calls from your creditors.

If you are unwilling to talk to your friends and your family about how much debt you really have, or if you're lying to them about it.

If you're worried about your debt.

You can't pay off your credit cards within a year using your income.

Sometimes we get deep into debt because we are trying to set ourselves up for the future. For example, taking out student loans to get through college, or furnishing your new house using a credit card or two.

Of course, there are those people who are addicted to shopping and purchasing things. Every shiny new object that passes their way must be bought, and it has to be purchased now.

Introduction

Then there are those who have addictions such as gambling, alcohol, cigarettes, drugs, and so forth. They use their credit to fund their addictions until they can no longer do so. When this happens, the addictions often force them to use less reputable ways to get money, including loan sharks, criminal behaviors, or selling themselves for unwholesome activities.

I've known people, as well, who were simply addicted to using credit cards. It wasn't that they wanted things, so much as they enjoyed using credit cards. Once they purchased the objects, they lost interest, either losing them or selling them. The objective was to buy on credit.

Medical problems can force a family deep into debt, even given such programs as Obamacare and other health insurance programs. This debt can come on suddenly, and is extended directly by hospitals and doctors rather than being put on credit cards. Sometimes these debts can force a family into bankruptcy whether they like it or not.

In all these cases, the first step is recognizing that you have a problem. You have to acknowledge that you are in debt – well beyond your means to pay it back within a year, two years, a decade, or even more. If you have addictions that are driving that debt, then you have an even larger problem to confront.

The place to start is to acknowledge that you have a debt problem. The second step is to be willing to do what you need to do to resolve that problem.

You may need to earn more income by working a second or even a third job, or starting a business from home. You could also talk to a consumer credit counseling service and come to an agreement with your creditors about how to repay your debt. Bankruptcy is always an option, although it should be done as a last resort.

Obviously, if you have addictions or bad habits driving the debt, then you may need to confront them as well. This can be made even more difficult if those addictions or bad habits involved a family member. It can be very difficult to solve addictions for other people, especially if they are not willing to confront them themselves.

Once you acknowledge that you're in debt, that the problem is affecting your life, and that you want to correct it, you need to take action.

The first thing to do is to take stock of your finances. It's a simple matter of making a spreadsheet, whether on paper or on a computer, of what money you have coming in and what money you have going out on a monthly basis. Money coming in from a credit card through a cash advance is not counted as money coming in.

You want to be clear when you're making this document which outgoing money is optional and which is mandatory. We'll discuss this in more detail later in this book.

This can be an eye-opening exercise, especially when you discover you have more going out then is coming in by a wide margin.

Once you know where you are financially – and there are a few more steps which we will discuss later – you can create a plan.

Introduction

Is it possible for you to get out of debt with your current income? If the answer is yes, how long will it take?

Do you need help managing your debt?

Is your debt situation so beyond hope that you need to think about bankruptcy?

It may be scary or even terrifying to look at the problem this closely. You may need to do it in small doses, or you may need some help from a friend or a counselor.

Regardless, your financial health, and perhaps even your sanity, depends on you getting through this exercise. Other members of your family may also be counting on you to bring this to a resolution.

This is intended to be a simple book, giving you straightforward tips on how to confront, understand, and handle your debt situation. The option of bankruptcy is always available, and if you're considering an option you need to seek a qualified legal professional. I will not be discussing the bankruptcy option within this book, as I'm not qualified to provide those answers.

When necessary, seek out the help of qualified professionals to validate the conclusions that you come to as you read through this book. It's important that you talk to your accountant, lawyer or other professional before implementing any of the steps outlined here.

I hope you enjoy what I've written and find it to be of some value. If you would like to send me a note about this book, feel free to write me at rich@thewritingking.com. If you enjoyed the book, please write a positive review

Worst Case Scenario

Credit cards are just too damn convenient. It seems so easy when you see something on sale, or that you like, to pull out a credit card and buy it. After all, it doesn't reduce your bank account balance any, right? And you can take years to pay it back, or even decades. Surely you'll be able to make the money to repay the debt way before then.

And besides, that fun little trinket or gift or book only cost $20.90. What harm could so little money cause? It's not like it's a fortune or anything.

Unfortunately, it all adds up, and before too long it's a major amount of money. But that's the way it starts, just a credit card, a few purchases, and you find out how easy it is to get those things you want or those gifts for someone else.

Then one day you find the credit card has maxed out, and your credit line is used up. So you apply for another one, and to your surprise not only do they grant it, but they give you a very large amount of credit. It could be more money than you thought was possible. Maybe enough for a down payment on a car or some new furniture.

Speaking of a car or new furniture, everybody needs that kind of thing right? So you go out to the car dealer, and wham you walk out of there in a few hours with a brand-new shiny automobile. How could you lose, it's only a $195 per month, right?

Worst Case Scenario

And you need that new furniture, so you walk into the furniture place. You intend to use your shiny new credit card with a large credit limit, but the furniture store has its own credit line. You decide to be smart – after all, why use up your new credit card? So you apply for the furniture store credit line and it's approved. In fact, they give you enough money not just to buy the new bed that you need, but to re-furnish your living room as well. So why not take advantage of that?

And so it goes, you get a gas card, and then another one from another station. Next, you get a couple of store cards, because you shop there all the time. It's really convenient, so why not?

At some point, you apply for a credit card, and it's declined. A letter comes in the mail claiming that your credit rating is low. How in the world can your credit rating be bad? You have over twenty credit cards after all. Doesn't that mean you have good credit?

You shrug, and apply for another card, but it's also declined. Again, the letter claims that your credit rating is too low.

Interesting, but it still probably is a fluke. You apply for a third one, because all your cards are maxed out, and you've come to depend on cash advances from them, and using that money for luxuries, groceries, gas, gifts, books, paintings, and anything else that you can find.

The third card is declined as well, and now you really begin to panic. What's going on? Don't they recognize that you pay your bills? You've never been late, after all, and isn't that what counts?

In desperation, you go down to your local bank to get an explanation. Surely it's all a mistake. All it will take as a talk with the manager to clear things up.

Tersely, the manager explains that you have too much debt in comparison to your income, and to make matters worse, all your cards are maxed out. In other words, you spent your entire credit limit of each and every one of your credit cards and credit lines. He's quite firm that you will not get any additional credit from his bank.

Desperation turns to panic. Your spending is more than your income,—when all the credit card payments are included. Actually, you have almost twice as much going out as you have coming in. The only way you been staying afloat is with the cash advances from new credit cards. But since those are no longer available, you are in deep trouble.

You keep applying for cards, and you manage to get a couple more, with outrageous interest charges. But that gives you a little breathing room, and you continue to use those cards to pay your other cards. Unfortunately, that only lasts for a few months, and the end result is that your pile of debt is even higher.

The inevitable happens and you find yourself missing a payment here and a payment there, because you simply don't make enough money to pay your rent, car payment, groceries, bills, and everything else.

Before long, you're paying a partial payment to some cards, and few are as far in arrears as 90 days. You start receiving

Worst Case Scenario

phone calls from the creditors. When are you going to pay them? Can you make a partial payment?

Your finances become truly desperate, and you miss a car payment, then another, and then another. Now you're getting calls from all of your creditors regularly – you know them all by name – and some of them are quite hostile. The bank holding the loan on your car is the worst of all.

In desperation, you change your phone number, but that doesn't stop the letters that pile up in your physical mailbox and your email inbox. Changing your email address fixes one problem, but you still receive as many as twenty letters in a single day. You dread every visit to your mailbox, which you sneak to late at night because you don't want anyone to know how bad the situation is for you.

You thought it couldn't get any worse, but one day a tow truck comes and takes away your car. You didn't know they could do that, but after an angry call to the bank, you find out that car loans are secured by the car itself. Since you haven't paid, the bank has every right to take it back. Now you're taking the bus to and from work every day.

You decide to look for a new job, one that makes more money. And lo and behold, a company invites you in for an interview. It all goes fine, and you fill out the paperwork without thinking anything about it. However, they turn you down for the job, in spite of being a perfect fit and the positive remarks from the interviewer. As it turns out, the company checked your credit, and denied you employment because of your credit record.

In despair, you think it's a good idea to move to a cheaper apartment, and you shop around until you find a place that's halfway decent. Again, you fill out the application, and are surprised that the apartment complex turns you down. Again, your bad credit record has caused the problem.

At this point, you look on the Internet and find a website which talks about various options that you have for getting out of debt. You schedule a virtual appointment (a meeting over the Internet) and wind up talking to a credit "professional."

After chatting with the man for two hours, he recommends a credit program and tells you you'll have to pay several thousand dollars up front. Once you do that, they will talk to their "insider contacts" and "make special deals with the credit card companies" to resolve your debt issue.

You pay the money, and the man comes back and tells you he needs more money to "smooth over a few things." With some further discussion, you realize that he's talking about passing around bribes. You're desperate, though, so you go ahead and pay the additional money.

Nothing happens for a week, and the man calls you back and says he has good news things are moving along. However, he needs a few thousand dollars... At this point, you stop him and tell him you have no more money.

He says you should borrow it from a family member – perhaps your father or mother can help. That makes sense, so you manage to get a goal from dad and pay it to the credit professional.

Worst Case Scenario

After that, you never hear from that man or the company again, and after a bit of research, you realize that you've been talking to a scammer. You just lost six thousand dollars of your hard-earned money. In fact, it was your entire savings. To make matters worse, you now also owe a few thousand dollars to your dad.

Finally, in desperation, you see a lawyer and talk to him about bankruptcy...

Admittedly, that's a worst-case scenario. Well, actually, things could get worse even than this. If you had an addiction or a bad habit such as gambling, you might reach out to a loan shark. That would lead to a far worse outcome than just seeing a bankruptcy lawyer or having your car repossessed.

In the rest of this book, we'll be discussing how you can come to grips with your debt situation, work out the severity of the problem, come up with a plan, and implement it until resolution.

Confronting the Problem

The very first thing you have to do when trying to handle any form of addiction, or when you're trying to resolve a problem, is to acknowledge the situation. If you don't do this, you'll never get started because you don't understand or believe that you have a problem.

Presumably, you're reading this book because you have, at least in the back of your mind, the thought that you need to handle your debt.

Perhaps your situation is grim or, alternately, your debt load is just larger than you're comfortable with and you feel it's time to get it taken care of.

Or possibly you have a loved one or a child or friend who's gotten themselves into trouble with debt, and you're wondering how to help them out. This is certainly true of many parents whose college age children have burdened themselves with phenomenal amounts of student loan debt.

In any event, the very first step that you have to take is the same step that is required for any kind of addiction or unwanted habit or characteristic.

You have to recognize it as a problem.

The second step is that you have to decide that the problem needs to be fixed, and it needs to be corrected beginning now.

Until you take those two steps, you are not going to get anything done.

Confronting the Problem

Sometimes it takes a good solid kick in the pants for people to do these two steps. It might require some harassing phone calls, your car being repossessed, a job being denied due to bad credit, or loan applications that fail to go through. The situation could even be so dire as to put your own freedom and living arrangements in danger.

Certainly, a mountain of debt can, at the very least, introduce a monumental amount of stress to your life.

A debt problem generally doesn't go away all by itself. Because of the way interest payments work, if you only pay the minimum, or less, your debt is going to take decades or longer to pay off.

This means that you're paying out large amounts of money in interest, which does nothing to pay off the principal of your debt. The principle is the amount of money that you owe, the interest is the money that banks, credit cards, and others charge you for the loan.

The interest payments incurred on a monthly basis make the process of getting out of debt even more difficult because this makes your monthly payments larger. Most of the money you pay won't go to help clear up your debt – you are just servicing your interest.

I know this sounds obvious, but the sooner you make the decision to handle the problem, the sooner you'll get yourself out of trouble. Putting it off doesn't help anyone except your creditors.

Once you confront the fact that you have a problem and decide to fix it, you're ready to go on to the next step which is determining how deep in the hole you really are. In other words, is the water up to your knees, your bellybutton, your neck, or over your head?

The In's and the Out's

Before you do anything else, it's important for you to stop using credit. This may be difficult because you may actually be surviving because of cash advances from your credit cards. However, as you work through the steps in this in the following chapters, one of your primary goals, if you do nothing else, is to be able to survive out of your income rather than your credit cards.

At this time your task is to figure out the magnitude of the problem. Chances are you've never really sat down and determined not just how deeply in debt you are, so now your job is to see how your debts compare with your income, savings, and other assets.

In simplest terms, you need to do an exercise to get a handle on how much money is coming in, how much you have on hand, and how much is going out. Before you can come up with any kind of realistic plan, you need this information.

Create a new spreadsheet in Excel or Google apps or some similar program, with one column for a description, money going out, and the third column is money coming in.

In the following sections, fill in the appropriate information in the spreadsheet.

INCOME

For many, it's probably pretty easy to figure out what's coming in, so it is a great place to start. Most people have a check (or more commonly direct deposit) coming periodically, once a month or every other week or once a week, from their job, double income houses may have two checks. If you're working more than one job take into account all of those sources of income.

Be sure you include all sources of income. Your paychecks, paychecks of other household family members, and any kind of consulting income, royalties, IRA payments, Social Security, and other money that you receive. Make note of when you receive those monies, weekly, biweekly, monthly or whatever.

Don't include any money you are not sure about receiving. If your uncle George owes you one thousand dollars and hasn't paid for couple years, don't include it as income. Chances are you're never going to get paid.

RESERVES

Next, make a list of all of the money that you have as assets or reserves, this would include equity on your home, equity in your car, savings, or anything else that has a reasonable amount of liquidity. By that I mean you can get to the asset or liquidated (for example sell your home) within a relatively short amount of time.

You can also make a list of longer-term assets, such as bonds, but keep it separate because you can't get to that money right away.

I'm not going to discuss reserves much in this book, except to say that you may find you could sell your house, cash out some bonds, or dig into your savings to get the money to pay off your debt.

DEBTS

Next, list out all of your debts. Be sure to include everything: credit cards, medical debts, loans from friends and family, mortgage payments, car payments, furniture payments, store cards, and anything else that would count as debt.

One way to get this information is to look over your checkbook or the online equivalent from your bank, your credit card statements, and so forth.

Separate this list into secured and unsecured debts. Secure debts include your home, your car, and probably furniture and so forth. Unsecured debts are credit cards and lines of credit. Note that some credit cards and lines of credit are secured, so you might have to look at the contracts.

Optionally, and this will be an eye-opener, include on each line item the total amount of interest per payment. Interest can vary month to month, so just use the numbers from your current set of statements. This will tell you how much money you're flushing down the toilet every single month. It does nothing for you except drain your money.

EXPENSES

Finally, make a list of all of your recurring expenses. This includes your utilities, rent, insurances, child support and so on. Make a notation next to each item indicating whether or not it's mandatory. For example, paying the electric bill and

The In's and the Out's

child support is mandatory, but some of your insurances may be worth looking at to see if you really need them.

Be sure to include any expenses that are quarterly or yearly as well and note the dates. Some insurance payments or once a year or once every six months, and they need to be taken into account.

Now create line items for consumables. This includes food, gasoline, car repairs, diapers, and so forth. You might have to make estimates of the amount you spend. List each major type of consumable as a separate line item.

List anything that would qualify as a vice or an addiction with estimates of how much you spend per month on each one. This would include cigarettes, alcohol, pornography, gambling, and other similar things that cost you money on a regular basis. For example, if you smoke a pack of cigarettes a day, and those cost $5 each, then you would put $150 for the amount.

ADD IT ALL UP

Add up all the money going out, and compare it to the money coming in. Do you have more money going out then you have coming in? Depending on the answer to that question, and the severity of the issue, you'll need to look at raising more income, cutting expenses or both.

Getting More Income

As you go through the exercise of figuring out how to work yourself out of debt, keep in mind that there are two sides to the picture: income and debt. You always want to look at both sides and do what you can to improve the situation in both directions.

Do you have any options for getting more income? This can be important for digging yourself out of debt.

Can you work a second job? One option is to find another job and work in the night or on weekends.

Can your spouse or other members of your family either work or work in a second job? If you have young adults at home, high school age or higher, one option is to get them employed in bringing in income. If they are living at home, you can ask them to help out by working another job and contributing part of their income to help the family.

Can you work from home? There are many opportunities for creating income available on the Internet. Be careful about spending any money on any kind of "get rich" schemes — let me tell you a little secret, they are virtually all scams.

Can you sell some of your belongings? If you're like many people, over the years you've built up collections of many different things that seemed, at the time, to be important. One option is to review what you own and sell what you can on eBay or local swap meets.

Getting More Income

It's important to understand that any kind of criminal activity of any form is not appropriate for getting out of debt.

You see, in the United States, you can't go to prison for being in debt. Your life can become uncomfortable, and it can become difficult to buy things, but nobody can put you in jail for not paying your debts.

Thus, there is no need, nor should you even consider, criminal activities to resolve your debt problem.

Cutting the Vices

If you are honest when you put together your spreadsheet of your income and expenses, you noted a few addictions or vices. Be sure to consider everything including those debts of any family members or anyone else that you are supporting.

Now you're going to have to ask yourself a tough question: can you stop doing one or more of these vices or addictions?

It's important to confront this if you're in a debt situation because what that means is you are spending money on your addictions or vices where the money could be better served towards balancing your budget or paying down the debt.

If you are gambling, you'll have to stop if you want to get out of debt. Gambling might be the reason why you're in debt in the first place, and if you want to resolve the issue, you have to resolve the gambling. You may find that you have to handle a gambling addiction before you can even attempt to get out of debt.

If you are a shopaholic, or you make purchases from those Home Shopping Network type shows on a regular basis, or you're addicted to infomercials, in order to get out of debt you'll need to break those habits. Stop doing them. To be successful, you might need to get rid of your cable entirely.

Addictive vices such as smoking, drinking, and drugs have physical withdrawal symptoms that may make it difficult, if not impossible, to stop those vices entirely while you're under the stress of handling your debt.

Cutting the Vices

If you have one or more of these addictions, you may find it better to try to cut down the amount that you're doing as opposed to stopping entirely. For example, if you are smoking two packs of cigarettes a day, perhaps you can, over the course of a few weeks, cut it down to just one pack per day. Or if you're drinking a six pack of beer every day, you might try to lower that just two or three bottles.

Whatever the vice, and most people have at least one, examine it and decide what steps you can take to reduce your expenses in that area.

You'll also need to go through the same exercise with any family members or friends that are reliant on your income.

Cutting Expenses

Now it's time to address your expenses. In this section, I'm going to go through a few areas where you can reduce expenses and give you some examples of how to do that. Keep in mind this is just the beginning, and you can do a lot more using these as examples as a starting point.

Keep in mind that legal commitments such as child support are not optional. Regardless of your financial situation, child support should be near or at the top of your list of things to pay. I specifically mention child support because not only is there a legal commitment but there's also an ethical and moral requirement that you pay to support your own children.

Your objective is to go through your expenses is to find those things that you can live without and stop paying for them.

A common expense that most people don't even think twice about is eating out at restaurants and fast food. You can cut your expenses dramatically by eating at home instead of going out to restaurants.

Another tactic, if you're already eating at home, is to examine the types of foods and toiletries and such that you are purchasing. Are using brand names? Take a look at the store or off brands and compare prices. You may find that you can save a substantial amount of money by eliminating the higher-priced brand names from your diet.

You can save money by examining your toiletries. Brand names of toilet paper and paper towels can cost 50% or even

Cutting Expenses

100% more than the off brands. Additionally, if you're purchasing things like paper plates, plastic knives, and forks, and so forth you can save by using reusable silverware, glasses, and plates.

Many Americans purchase a cup of coffee each morning, perhaps at lunch or even dinner. It seems to have become routine for individuals to spend $5 a day or so at their local Starbucks or the equivalent – if you do the math, you'll find that $5 a day for 30 days (one month) is $150, or $1,800 a year! That's an insane amount of money to be spending on coffee. This should be one of the first things that you cut out of your lifestyle to help handle you're debt. For the same price as that cup of coffee, you can easily buy enough coffee beans to make 30 cups at home.

I'm sure you can see the general pattern that's emerging. It's quite common for people not to have a handle on this kind of spending. After all, it's just five dollars to buy that cup of coffee, $6.71 for that pack of cigarettes or $1.25 for the candy bar – and it's likely you are not keeping track of these expenditures.

Carry a small notepad with you or use a simple notepad type application on your cell phone. As you go through the day, making purchases, note them down, and do this for at least a week; better yet for several months. As you make these notations, you'll notice patterns emerging. You'll see that you, for example, purchase a cup of coffee every morning from a local Starbucks, then you get a sandwich from Subway's, followed by a pack of gum, and finally you stop for a 64 ounce soda from the gas station on the way home.

Adding all these items up, you might see that you are spending $20, $30 or even more every single day on these "minor" regular purchases. In a thirty day month, your expenditures for these items can be close to a thousand dollars.

Add to this the cost of eating out, which is common to many individuals and families these days, and you may be spending another thousand dollars a month (or more for a family) for restaurant and fast food.

As you create your list, and the patterns become obvious, you're going to face some choices. Is that $5 cup of coffee every day, totaling $150 a month, important? Or would it be better for you to buy a bag of coffee from the store once a month for twenty bucks?

Even a dollar every day for a pack of gum as up quickly. You can make a huge dent in your expenditures by going through this exercise.

GROCERY STORES
When you go to the supermarket to buy groceries make a list of everything that you purchase along with the brand name and price. While you're shopping, compare that brand name to the store brand or other brands of the same or similar items.

You might find that you are spending two or three times as much to fill your shopping cart as you would if you spent some time looking for lower cost items.

Switching supermarkets can also save you money, and alternately, you can shop at two, three or even four

Cutting Expenses

supermarkets to get the best deals at each one. For example, you might pick up milk and eggs from one because they are on special, bread from another, and produce from a third. This is a great way to take advantage of specials and coupons.

Don't forget about dollar stores for paper goods, supplies, cleaning items, and so forth.

Another tip is to stay away from shopping for food when you are hungry. I don't know about you, but if I go into the supermarket with an empty tummy, I will wind up spending quite a bit more on food than if I'd gone after dinner.

Have you ever noticed that if you go to the store just to pick up one item you wind up purchasing a lot more than you intended? After all, it seems like such a wasted trip to just pick up a single loaf of bread, so why not by an extra dozen eggs or six pack of soda or something else? Grocery stores and supermarkets depend on that mentality.

To handle that problem, shop only once or twice a week, and prepare a list of everything you are going to purchase. Don't deviate from that list.

COUPONS
You might think that coupons are a great way to save money, but you need to keep in mind that manufacturers do not provide coupons to cut their profit. Coupons are a way to get you into the store to buy things, and their hope is that you add extra items to your shopping cart or purchase more than you normally would. Remember, every time that the supermarket

can get you back into the store, you are likely to make more purchases.

Some people engage in what's called extreme couponing; this means spending time to find coupons and combine them in such a way as to get massive discounts on purchases. Some people are so good at this that they wind up actually getting money back from the supermarket every time they make a "purchase." "-

Using coupons in this manner requires a lot of effort, and that time might be more wisely spent finding a second job or working to make income on the Internet or from home.

That being said, if you have a family member who is not working, one way they can contribute is to search the Internet, magazines, and newspapers (be careful not to spend much money on these) for bargains and coupons.

Loyalty cards are a form of an electronic coupon, and used wisely they can save you money. Be careful that you're not lured into purchasing more than you need just to get a "good price." Always remember that supermarkets are not in the business of saving you money or cutting their profits. Every price cut, every two-for-one special, every featured item, and everything on sale is intended to get you into the store so you make more purchases, and thus earn them more money.

UTILITIES AND INSURANCES

One task that can be very useful for cutting expenses is to go through each and every bill: utilities, insurances, credit cards, and even mortgages looking for things that can be reduced or cut entirely.

For example, the average car insurance premium includes a plethora of additional services such as emergency roadside assistance and towing. Cutting these things out of your policy can save you quite a few dollars each month or year.

For every insurance, it's a good idea to get on the phone with an agent to discuss each and every line item until you understand the purpose for every single charge. This can take as long as an hour or two for each one, but the results can lead to quite a savings.

When I performed this exercise, I was amazed at the number of extra services that had somehow slipped into my insurances that I really didn't need or want. Cutting these services or reducing them resulted in a savings of over a thousand dollars a year. Yes, it took several long phone calls, and a bit of searching to find the right person at each insurance company, but it was well worth the effort.

Remember, you are charged for these premiums every single month, quarter or year, and over time they can add up to quite a bit of money.

Perform the same exercise with your electric bill, and take the time to read one of your statements from top to bottom. For many electric companies, you can get price reductions or credits for low income or if you are having problems paying. Sometimes these are spelled out in your statements. Regardless, spend the time to have a long discussion with a service representative to find out what is optional and can be removed or reduced, and what options are available for low income or problem situations.

Your telephone bill can be very difficult to understand because they include lots of obscure charges, taxes, and tariffs. Discuss each and every one of these with a representative of your phone company to determine what can be reduced or eliminated.

Next, take a look at your cable or television bill. Do you really need to have all of those fancy options? Is it important to have access to five hundred different channels on TV? Discuss your options with your cable company's representatives and you may find that you can cut your bill down dramatically.

In fact, I make it a habit to call my cable company once a year, and each time they seem to find some "new" or "special" package for me with a reduced rate substantially less than I'd been paying. The general rule of thumb is if you don't call, you won't get the special rate.

Before you cancel anything, make sure there is not a cancellation charge. It can be quite a shock to cancel a cell phone and get whacked with a three hundred dollar charge because you terminated the contract early.

MEDICAL EXPENSES

There is no bigger shock, in my experience, than receiving a bill after spending some time in the hospital.

Those unexpected bills can be dramatic and very demoralizing. Even though the insurance may cover a significant amount, there may be thousands of dollars of charges that were partially or not covered at all.

This can make you feel helpless, but a change of attitude may save you quite a bit of that money.

You see, in this situation you actually have the power. The hospital, doctor or medical facility wants your money. Every month that you don't pay costs them in interest and collection charges. If the bill goes delinquent, and they have to sell it to a collection agency, they only get pennies on the dollar.

On several occasions, I had a discussion with a hospital billing specialist and have managed to sharply reduce or even on some instances to completely eliminate charges.

One trick is to tell the billing specialist that you'd be willing to pay a certain percentage of the bill today if they will accept it as paying off the entire amount. This doesn't always work, but if you find the right person and make the right offer, you may get lucky. You certainly will lose nothing by asking. If you go into this negotiation in a friendly and pleasant manner, and keep your cool, you may find them accepting 50%, 40%, or even less to pay off the entire amount.

Another aspect of this is to remember that just because one person says no doesn't mean the answer is no. You can always call a supervisor, manager, even a vice president. Sometimes, calling back and talking to the same person a few days later results in an entirely different outcome.

Note that being abrasive, abusive, demeaning, or upsetting will not aid you in this process. No one likes to be abused or yelled at, and doing so to the service representatives will cause them to flag you as a troublemaker, and you will find that you won't get any price reductions at all.

Just keep in mind that you have the power. They want your money, and you don't have to give it to them. No one's going to put you in jail for not paying a medical bill. Take this attitude, and go into your negotiations confident but friendly, and you may be pleasantly surprised to find out how far you can get.

A final note on medical bills, none of this works if the bill is sent to collections. Once your account has been sold to a collection agency, you're dealing with a whole different group of people. They paid money for that debt. Their purpose is to get as much back from you as they can.

HARD CHOICES

You may find yourself having to make some more difficult decisions in order to reduce your expenses.

For example, you might need to cancel vacation plans, transfer your children into public school, or get rid of that second car. You might find yourself eliminating insurances that you actually believe you need, delaying car repairs, wearing clothing longer than you're comfortable with, or purchasing fewer gifts for Christmas and birthdays.

Just remember that every dollar of debt you eliminate can save you several dollars in payments over a several year period due to interest charges. If you can create an extra three hundred dollars a month by making your own coffee, bringing lunch to work, and cutting back on your soda, and then apply that to your debt, you may find your situation improving very quickly.

Delaying sending a child to college, and saving the $20,000 tuition, could mean paying off a fair chunk of your debt quickly, and having more money to send them a year later. That would be a tough decision, but it may be something you need to confront.

CONCLUSION

An important step in cutting expenses is to identify and reduce or eliminate anything that you're paying that is unneeded or a luxury.

Even though I don't have a debt problem, I perform this exercise once a year because it's amazing how many expenses and charges creep in without any effort on my part. Thus, this is a useful exercise regardless of your financial situation.

Most people can easily find an extra few hundred or even a thousand dollars of "extra" money each month by simply going through anything they purchase a regular basis and making some rational changes.

Things you shouldn't do

As you are working to clear up your debt, there are a number of things that you should be careful about doing.

I want to stress again, and I've mentioned it already, that under no circumstances (unless, of course, you are living on the street) should you even consider reducing or not paying your child support. Responsible adults fulfill their legal, moral and ethical responsibilities to their children, regardless of the difficulties of the situation they find themselves in.

You might think that you can save a lot of money by moving to a cheaper apartment, but that's generally something you should consider as a last resort. Moving can be very upsetting and depressing, and will take a lot of time and effort. It will also cost money to rent a truck, possibly hire somebody to help you move, and so forth. Finally, if your credit record has been damaged, you may even find it difficult to find another apartment willing to accept you.

Never, ever miss paying your rent. Rental history goes on a national database which can be accessed by any apartment manager. This is separate from your credit record.

This should go without saying, but don't do anything illegal or unethical. This will always catch up with you, and will put you in a far worse situation than merely being in debt. Remember, in the United States, you cannot be put in jail for not paying your debt. So don't even consider doing anything that might get you put in jail to pay off something that isn't illegal. Does that make sense?

Things you shouldn't do

I shouldn't have to mention this, but avoid loan sharks and super high interest lines of credit. These will come back to bite you hard so it's best to avoid them altogether.

Do not give into despair or depression and start or increase drinking, smoking, cigarettes, gambling or other vices to "make yourself feel better." These kinds of activities not only will make you feel worse, they will deepen the problem and make it even more difficult to get out of debt.

Other Things to do

You may be thinking at this point in time that making so many cuts in your expenses and the money you spend is going to eliminate all of the fun from your life.

After all, you enjoy drinking a cup of coffee from Starbucks each morning, yet now it seems you have to eliminate it entirely.

It might appear that all of the things that you enjoy in life, things that you been doing for years to help cope with the hardships, to relieve stress, and to feel better about yourself, can no longer be done. How will you cope now?

Believe it or not, there are many activities available to you that cost little to no money.

Did you know there is actually no need to ever pay for a movie or a book? Virtually every city has public libraries which loan CDs, DVDs, and books. Just get a library card, and you will be welcome to borrow these and read or watch them in the comfort of your home. This simple step can eliminate the need for Netflix or other subscription services.

Cities always have public parks and botanical gardens which you can visit, often times for free. In the case of botanical gardens, on most days there's a small charge, but they usually have a free day or two every month.

You can always go hiking and take walks. In fact, while you're going through the stress of getting yourself out of debt, getting

Other Things to do

outdoors and walking is very wise. This activity can go a long way towards fending off anxiety and depression.

The local YMCA or similar organizations have many different programs and activities for a small monthly fee of just a few dollars.

In fact, I would recommend considering this an opportunity for you to explore the options available to you and your family for little or no charge. You may be pleasantly surprised at discovering how much you can do without any more money than the cost of the gasoline or bus fare to get there.

Another option, which I also heartily recommend, is to volunteer to help in various organizations, even if only for a few hours a week. These don't pay any money, of course, but they will get you out in the world with people, which can be great therapy. Giving and helping can also go a long way towards reducing stress and making you feel better about yourself because it gets your mind off of you and your problems.

While you are working through your debt problem, you may find yourself under more stress than normal. People under stress are more likely to be ill, have accidents, and make mistakes. Take great care to eat healthy foods, exercise, get out into the fresh air, and avoid negative people. These things will help you improve your situation and fight off the negative feelings.

Social media

Take this opportunity to go through all of your social media accounts – Facebook, for example – and clean them up. Employers, apartment managers, insurance agents, and everyone else frequently search the Internet for information about applicants before granting credit, hiring, and so forth.

Inappropriate photos of drinking and other shenanigans, heated political posts, and other materials that make you look less than professional can damage your reputation and your chances of getting what you want in the world.

If you're not already a member of LinkedIn, get on the site and create an account. Fill in the information to make yourself look good, to attract potential employers, and to give those who are searching for you on the Internet positive information about you.

This will give those who search on the internet to find out about you something positive to find.

Consumer Credit Counseling

You may need help with these steps, or you may find that after you've done them you still don't have enough room in your budget to pay the bills and survive.

Many people feel ashamed at getting themselves deeply in debt, and hesitate to visit a consumer credit counselor because of that. Don't let your emotions stop you – counselors see these kinds of problems all day long, and they are trained to help you.

Consumer credit counselors can help you come to terms with your debt. Their mission is to work with you and your creditors to come up with a plan that works in your situation.

One of the advantages of getting on a consumer credit counseling program is they can get the majority of your creditors — for unsecured loans only — to reduce or eliminate the interest charges while you're on the plan. Additionally, they will negotiate with your creditors for reduced monthly payment terms.

This can help you in more ways than you think. Of course the monthly payments are reduced, but additionally, since the interest charges are removed you're paying towards the principal and not wasting money paying interest charges. This will get you out of debt faster.

Why do credit card companies deal with consumer credit counselors? Because they do not want you missing payments, charging off your account, or declaring bankruptcy.

Consumer Credit Counseling

All of those things are expensive for the banks, and if they can cut you a break, using the counselor as a mediator, and ensure that you will pay off your debt, they are ahead of the game.

Generally, you wind up paying one payment to the consumer credit counseling agency each month. They will distribute that amount to all of your creditors. There will be a charge for the counseling services each month, but the total that you wind up paying will be less than which were paying before in most cases.

SETTLEMENT PROGRAMS

I would highly recommend against joining a settlement program. These are explained by unscrupulous companies as a great way to get yourself out of debt quickly. Unfortunately, in most cases, they are lying. Settlement programs devastate your credit for years to come.

The way a settlement program works is your "counselor" will tell you to stop paying any payments to all of your credit cards that are within the plan. They will ask you to sign powers of attorney to give them some power over negotiating your debts. Generally, you'll have to sign one for each debt.

Your credit card companies will be informed to send all calls over to your program representatives. This does have the advantage of eliminating the harassing calls.

Most of these plans require you to pay a certain amount into the plan each month, which goes into a "savings" account. This is to be used to pay off your debts when the time comes.

After a period of about six months, some of your credit card companies will call and start making offers for a reduced payment amount. Your program representatives have a good understanding of just how far these credit card companies will go, and will hold out for better rates.

The idea is that a credit card company might offer your debt to be paid off if you pay them 60% of the loan immediately. Sometimes though go down as low as 25%. It all depends on the credit card company, and how long the amounts been in arrears.

So far it all sounds pretty good, right?

Actually, this devastates your credit rating. All of these cards will show up on your credit report as extremely delinquent, and when you pay them off, they will often be shown as paid charge-offs. These remain on your credit record for around seven years. They will prevent you from getting additional credit for that time period.

The second thing that is in the fine print of the contract will say, but that you probably will miss, is that the difference between the loan amounts in the amount you pay is taxable immediately in the current year.

For example, if you had a credit card debt with a bank for $10,000, and were able to negotiate an immediate $4,000 to forgive the loan, you would be responsible for paying the tax on $6,000 in that year.

Consumer Credit Counseling

As you can see, this can dramatically increase your tax bill. In the tax, men tend to be a lot less forgiving about payment than credit card companies.

I would advise extreme caution before accepting or even considering a settlement program.

BANKRUPTCY

Obviously, there may come a point when you need to consider bankruptcy. Because I'm not an attorney or accountant, I'm going to stop here and recommend that if you're at this point, you seek professional help.

.

Conclusion

Getting in over their heads in debt is a problem that many people and families have to confront during their lives. This can happen because of poor spending habits, vices, addictions, loss of employment, medical problems, unexpectedly large bills, and other life circumstances.

You can choose to be a victim of the problem or take the time to understand your situation, get a grasp of all of your income and expenses, come up with a plan to get out of debt, implement the plan and work through it.

Consumer credit counselors exist to help people in these situations confront their debt and create a plan to handle it. These counselors have the support of credit card companies and banks because it's to everyone's advantage to work it out.

One of the most important things that you can do to resolve your debt situation is to identify and reduce or eliminate any expenses due to addictions or vices, as well as any optional or unneeded expenditures. Sometimes even eliminating that pack of gum each day or cutting your drinking habit in half can have a huge effect on the amount of money available.

Keep in mind that there are many options for entertainment available to you for free or little charge. Take advantage of these to help you reduce your stress, fight depression, and feel better about yourself. Don't forget about the possibility of volunteering, even for a few hours a week, as this can do a lot to help with self-esteem.

Conclusion

You can get out of debt if you can work out and follow a comprehensive plan. Now is as good as any time to get started.

Before you go

If you scroll to the last page in this eBook, you will have the opportunity to leave feedback and share the book with Before You Go. I'd be grateful if you turned to the last page and shared the book.

Also, if you have time, please leave a review. Positive reviews are incredibly useful. If you didn't like the book, please email me at rich@thewritingking.com and I'd be happy to get your input.

linkedin.thewritingking.com

About the Author

<https://www.linkedin.com/in/richardlowejr>
Feel free to send a connection request

Follow me on Twitter: @richardlowejr

Richard Lowe has leveraged more than 35 years of experience as a Senior Computer Manager and Designer at four companies into that of a bestselling author, blogger, ghostwriter, and public speaker. He has written hundreds of articles for blogs and ghostwritten more than a dozen books and has published manuscripts about computers, the Internet, surviving disasters, management, and human rights. He is currently working on a ten-volume science fiction series – the Peacekeeper Series – to be published at the rate of three volumes per year, beginning in 2016.

Richard started in the field of Information Technology, first as the Vice President of Consulting at Software Techniques, Inc. Because he craved action, after six years he moved on to work for two companies at the same time: he was the Vice President of Consulting at Beck Computer Systems and the Senior Designer at BIF Accutel. In January 1994, Richard found a home at Trader Joe's as the Director of Technical Services and Computer Operations. He remained with that incredible company for almost 20 years before taking an early retirement to begin a new life as a professional writer. He is currently the CEO of The Writing King, a company that provides all forms of writing services, the owner of The EBay King, and a Senior Branding Expert for LinkedIn Makeover. You can find a current list of all books on his Author Page and

About the Author

take a look at his exclusive line of coloring books at The Coloring King.

Richard has a quirky sense of humor and has found that life is full of joy and wonder. As he puts it, "This little ball of rock, mud, and water we call Earth is an incredible place, with many secrets to discover. Beings fill our corner of the universe, and some are happy, and others are sad, but each has their unique story to tell."

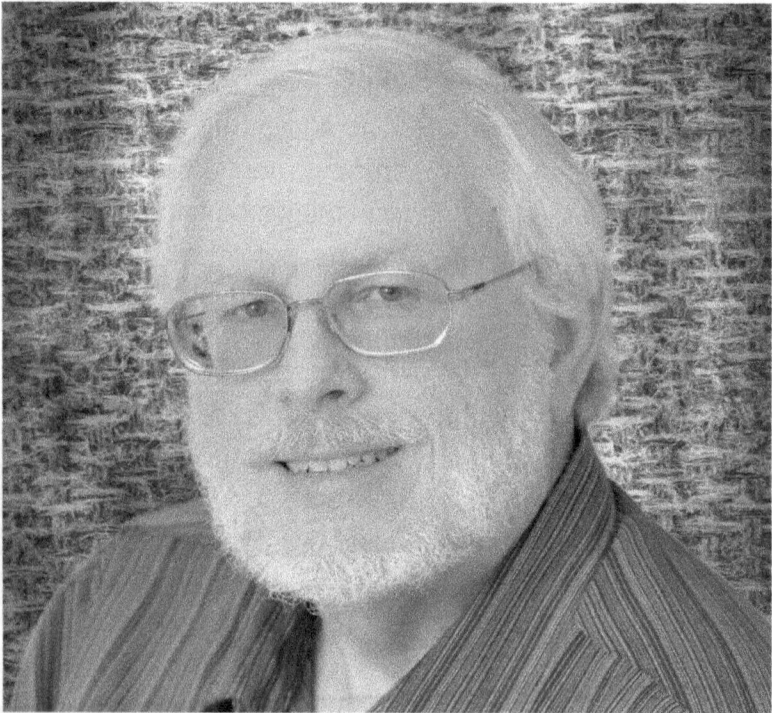

His philosophy is to take life with a light heart, and he approaches each day as a new source of happiness. Evil is ignored, discarded, or defeated; good is helped, enriched, and fulfilled. One of his primary interests is to educate people about their human rights and assist them to learn how to be happy in life.

Richard spent many happy days hiking in national parks, crawling over boulders, and peering at Indian pictographs. He toured the Channel Islands off Santa Barbara and stared in fascination at wasps building their homes in Anza-Borrego. One of his joys is photography, and he has photographed more than 1,200 belly dancing events, as well as dozens of Renaissance fairs all over the country.

Because writing is his passion, Richard remains incredibly creative and prolific; each day he writes between 5,000 and 10,000 words, diligently using language to bring life to the world so that others may learn and be entertained.

Richard is the CEO of The Writing King, which specializes in fulfilling any writing need. You can find out more at https://www.thewritingking.com/, and emails are welcome at rich@thewritingking.com

Books by Richard G Lowe Jr.

Business Professional Series

On the Professional Code of Ethics and Business Conduct in the Workplace – Professional Ethics: 100 Tips to Improve Your Professional Life - have you ever wondered what it takes to be successful in the professional world? This book gives you some tips that will improve your job and your career.

Help! My Boss is Whacko! - How to Deal with a Hostile Work Environment - sometimes the problem is the boss. There are all kinds of managers, some competent, some incompetent, and others just plain whacked. This book will help you understand and handle those different types of managers.

Help! I've Lost My Job: Tips on What to do When You're Unexpectedly Unemployed – suddenly having to leave your job can be a harsh and emotional time in your life. Learn some of the things that you need to consider and handle if this happens to you.

Help! My Job Sucks Insider Tips on Making Your Job More Satisfying and Improving Your Career – sometimes conditions conspire to make the regular trek to a job feel like a trip through Dante's Inferno. Sometimes, these are out of our control, such as a malicious manager or incompetent colleague. On the other hand, we can take control of our lives and workplace and improve our situation. Get this book to learn what you can do when your job sucks.

45

Books by Richard G Lowe Jr.

How to Manage a Consulting Project: Make money, get your project done on time, and get referred again and again – I found that being a consultant is a great way to earn a living. Managing a consulting project can be a challenge. This book contains some tips to help you so you can deliver a better product or service to your customers.

How to be a Good Manager and Supervisor, and How to Delegate – Lessons Learned from the Trenches: Insider Secrets for Managers and Supervisors – I've been a manager for over thirty years I learned many things about how to get the job done and deliver quality service. The information in this book will help you manage your projects to a high level of quality.

Focus on LinkedIn – Learn how to create a LinkedIn profile and to network effectively using the #1 business social media site.

Home Computer Security Series

Safe Computing is Like Safe Sex: You have to practice it to avoid infection – Security expert and Computer Executive, Richard Lowe, presents the simple steps you can take to protect your computer, photos and information from evil doers and viruses. Using easy-to-understand examples and simple explanations, Lowe explains why hackers want your system, what they do with your information, and what you can do to keep them at bay. Lowe answers the question: how to you keep yourself say in the wild west of the internet.

Books by Richard G Lowe Jr.

<u>Disaster Preparation and Survival Series</u>

<u>Real World Survival Tips and Survival Guide: Preparing for and Surviving Disasters with Survival Skills</u> – CERT (Civilian Emergency Response Team) trained and Disaster Recovery Specialist, Richard Lowe, lays out how to make you, your family, and your friends ready for any disaster, large or small. Based upon specialized training, interviews with experts and personal experience, Lowe answers the big question: what is the secret to improving the odds of survival even after a big disaster?

<u>Creating a Bug Out Bag to Save Your Life: What you need to pack for emergency evacuations</u> - When you are ordered to evacuate—or leave of your free will—you probably won't have a lot of time to gather your belongings and the things you'll need. You may have just a few minutes to get out of your home. The best preparation for evacuation is to create what is called a bug out bag. These are also known as go-bags, as in, "grab it and go!"

<u>Professional Freelance Writer Series</u>

<u>How to Operate a Freelance Writing Business, and How to be a Ghostwriter – Proven Tips and Tricks Every Author Needs to Know about Freelance Writing: Insider Secrets from a Professional Ghostwriter</u> – This book explains how to be a ghostwriter, and gives tips on everything from finding customers to creating a statement of work to delivering your final product.

<u>How to Write a Blog That Sells and How to Make Money From Blogging: Insider Secrets from a Professional Blogger:</u>

Books by Richard G Lowe Jr.

Proven Tips and Tricks Every Blogger Needs to Know to Make Money – There is an art to writing an article that prompts the reader to make a decision to do something. That's the narrow focus of this book. You will learn how to create an article that gets a reader interested, entices them, informs them, and causes them to make a decision when they reach the end.

Other Books by Richard Lowe Jr

How to Be Friends with Women: How to Surround Yourself with Beautiful Women without Being Sleazy – I am a photographer and frequently find myself surrounded by some of the most beautiful women in the world. This book explains how men can attract women and keep them as friends, which can often lead to real, fulfilling relationships.

How to Throw Parties like a Professional: Tips to Help You Succeed with Putting on a Party Event – Many of us have put on parties, and I know it can be a daunting and confusing experience. In this book, I share what I learned from hosting small house parties to shows and events.

Additional Resources

Is your career important to you? Find out how to move your career in any direction you desire, improve your long-term livelihood, and be prepared for any eventuality. Visit the page below to sign up to receive valuable tips via email, and to get a free eBook about how to optimize your LinkedIn profile.

http://list.thewritingking.com/

I've written and published many books on a variety of subjects. They are all listed on the following page.

https://www.thewritingking.com/books/

On that site, I also publish articles about business, writing, and other subjects. You can visit by clicking the following link:

https://www.thewritingking.com

To find out more about me or my photography, you can visit these sites:

Personal website: https://www.richardlowe.com
Photography: http://www.richardlowejr.com
LinkedIn Profile: https://www.linkedin.com/in/richardlowejr
Twitter: https://twitter.com/richardlowejr

If you have any comments about this book, feel free to email me at rich@thewritingking.com

Premium Writing Services

Do you have a story that needs to be told? Have you been trying to write a book for ages but never can seem to find the time to get it done? Do you want to brand your business, but don't know how to get started?

The Writing King has the answer. We can help you with any of your writing needs.

Ghostwriting. We can write your book, which entails interviewing you to get your story, writing the book and then working with you to revise it until complete. To discuss your book, contact The Writing King today.

Website Copy. Many businesses include the text on their sites as an afterthought, and that can result in lost sales and leads. Hire The Writing King to review your site and recommend changes to the text which will help communicate your message and improve your sales.

Blogging. Build engagement with your customers by hiring us to write a weekly or semi-weekly article for your blog, LinkedIn or other social media. Contact The Writing King today to discuss your blogging needs.

LinkedIn. LinkedIn is of the most important vehicles for finding new business, and a professionally written profile works to pulling in those leads. Write or update your profile today.

Technical Writing. We have broad experience in the computer, warehousing and retail industries, and have

Premium Writing Services

written hundreds of technical documents. Contact The Writing King today to find out how we can help you with your technical writing project.

The Writing King has the skills and knowledge to help you with any of your writing needs. Call us today to discuss how we can help you.